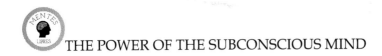

THE *POWER*

OF THE

SUBCONSCIOUS

MIND

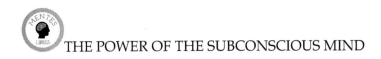

INDEX

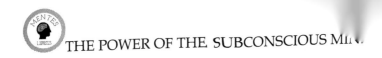

We begin...

This book instructs you on what to do and how to do it when it comes to harnessing and utilizing the powers of your subconscious.

Where have you been educated to use, neutralize, order or harmonize constructively with your passions, emotions, instincts, dispositions, feelings, moods and habits of idea and action?

Have you been instructed in how to aim high and achieve your goals regardless of obstacles? If your answer is "No". You will be taught these things if you read and then apply the precepts of this book.

Where this all starts

There is an invisible talisman (mental attitude) that has two amazing powers: it has the power to attract wealth, success, happiness and well-being; and it has the power to push back these things - to rob you of everything that makes life worth living.

It is the first of these powers, which allows a few men to climb to the top and stay there. It is the second that keeps other men at the bottom of their lives. It is the latter that drags other men from the top when they have achieved it.

A place to start

You must learn to develop the habit of recognizing, relating to, assimilating and using the universal precepts and adopting them as your own. Then go ahead with the desired action.

And what precepts could you apply? They can be learned and applied by young people and adults:

Greatness comes to those who acquire an ardent desire to achieve high goals.

Success is achieved and maintained by those who try to move forward with a positive mental attitude.

To become an expert in any human action requires practice... practice... practice... practice... practice.

Effort and work can become fun once desirable goals are set.

With each adversity there is a seed of an equivalent or better benefit for those who are motivated with a positive mental attitude to be successful.

The greatest power of man resides in the power of prayer.

To learn and apply these precepts, tune your invisible talisman to the side of the positive

mental attitude.

We are the masters of our destiny as we are, first, of our attitudes. Our attitudes determine our future. This is a universal law. This law works whether attitudes are destructive or constructive. The law says that we translate into physical truth the thoughts and attitudes we have in our brains, no matter what they are.

We translate into truth thoughts of poverty as quickly as we do with thoughts of wealth. But if our attitude toward ourselves is great, and our attitude toward other people is generous and merciful, we will

Draw large, generous portions of success.

As we well know, those who trust them cannot repel the positive; they use the negative side of their talisman. Those who trust them can repel the negative; they use the positive side.

That is why we must be cautious when using these talismans. Your positive side of mental attitude can get you all the rich blessings of life. It will help you overcome your problems and discover your strengths. It can help you get ahead of your rivals and make real what others say is impossible.

But negative mental attitude is just as powerful. Instead of happiness and success, it can attract despair and defeat. Like all power, the talisman is unsafe if we don't use

it the right way.

But how can you put a positive mental attitude to work in your life instead of a negative mental attitude? Some individuals seem to use this power instinctively. Some learn by relating and absorbing what they read in inspiring magazines and books.

Some individuals use a positive mental attitude for a while, but when they suffer a setback, they lose faith in it. They start well, but a few "fault breaks" turn the talisman around. They never realize that success is maintained by those who continue to deal with a positive mental attitude.

A few individuals seem to use a positive mental attitude almost all the time.

Other people start and then quit smoking. But other people - the vast majority of us - have never begun to use the fantastic powers at our disposal.

What about us? Can we learn to use the positive mental attitude, like we've learned other skills?

The answer, based on years of experience, is a definite yes.

This is the content of this book. In the following chapters we will show you how it can be done. The effort of learning will be worth it because positive mental attitude is the crucial ingredient for success.

You can alter your life

Now we know that a positive mental attitude is a big deal. Once you begin to employ these principles with a positive mental attitude in your preferred occupation or a solution to your personal problems, you are on the road to success. Then you are on the right path and you are going in the right direction to get what you want.

To achieve something worthwhile in life, it is crucial that you employ a positive mental attitude, no matter what other rules of success you employ.

The positive mental attitude is the catalyst

that makes any combination of precepts of success work for a worthwhile ending. Their negative mental attitude, combined with some of the same precepts, is the catalyst that results in crime or evil. And the pain, the calamity, the tragedy.

- Sin, sickness, death - these are some of its rewards.

The things you need

As long as you live, as of today, you will be able to analyze all your successes and all your failures, that is to say, if you form these principles indelibly in your memory.

You can develop and maintain a permanent

positive mental attitude by making it your duty to adopt and apply these principles in your daily life.

There is no other known technique by which you can keep your mind positive.

Analyze yourself courageously, now, and learn which of these precepts you have been using and which of them you have been overlooking.

In the future examine your successes and your charms, using the principles as a measuring system, and very soon you will be able to put your finger on what has been holding you back.

If you have a positive mental attitude and you don't succeed, then what? If you use a positive mental attitude and are unsuccessful, it may be because you are not using it in the right way in the combination for success to achieve your particular goal.

Initially it may be difficult to understand and apply the principles.

However, as you continue to read each of these precepts they will become clearer to you. Then you will be able to use them.

Has the world given you unfair treatment? "I never had the opportunity to move forward. My father was an alcoholic. "I grew up in the slum, and that's something you can never get out of your system."I only had a primary

education.

All these individuals are claiming, in essence, that the world has treated them unfairly. They blame the world and external conditions for their failures. They blame their inheritance or their environment. They begin with a negative mental attitude. And, naturally, with that attitude, they are disabled. But it is the negative mental attitude that is holding them back, not the strange disadvantage they provide as the cause of their failure.

Identifying oneself with a mental image of success can help break the habits of doubt and defeat the years of negative mental attitude established within a personality. A different and equally crucial strategy for altering your world is to identify with a mental image that will inspire you to make the right decisions. It can be a slogan, an image or any other symbol that is meaningful to you.

What will your image tell you? There is a way to find out. When faced with a serious issue or decision, ask your photograph a question. Listen, for the answer.

A different crucial ingredient to altering your world is having a definite purpose.

The definition of purpose is the starting point of all accomplishment.

The definition of purpose, combined with a positive mental attitude, is the starting point for all the accomplishments that are worth remembering - your world will alter whether or not you decide to alter it.

- However, you have the power to decide your direction. You can choose your own goals. When you determine your ultimate primary goals with a positive mental attitude, there is a natural tendency for you to use

Seven of the precepts of success:

- Personal initiative
- Self-control
- Original vision
- Organized thinking
- Commanded attention (concentration of efforts)

- Time and cash budgeting
- Exuberance

Goals

98 out of every 100 individuals who are unhappy with their world do not have a clear picture in their brains of the world they would like for themselves.

Consider it! Consider the individuals who wander aimlessly through life, discontented, struggling with many things, but without a clear goal. Can you say, right now, what do you want from life?

Setting your goals may not be easy. It may even involve a little painful self-contemplation. But it will be worth whatever work it takes, because as soon as you can name your goal, you can expect to enjoy many advantages. These advantages are almost automatic.

The first amazing advantage is that your subconscious begins to work under a universal law: "What the mind of man can conceive and believe - the mind of man can achieve with a positive mental attitude. Because you visualize your specified destiny, your subconscious is affected by this self-suggestion. He gets to work to help you get there.

Because you know what you want, there is a tendency for you to try to get to the right track and head in the right direction. You take action.

Work is now fun. You are motivated to pay the price. You budget your time and money. You give to books, think and plan. The more you consider your goals, the more enthusiastic you get. And with enthusiasm your desire becomes an ardent desire.

You receive alerts of opportunities that will help you achieve your goals as they arise in your daily experiences. Because you know what you want, you are more likely to recognize these opportunities.

All of these things are essential to a positive mindset and, consequently, to success.

Personal initiative

Consider something you want to accomplish that is really important to you? (Don't go ahead without choosing one of your main goals.) Now imagine having achieved it. You're enjoying the rewards of a job well done. What does it look like? What does it taste like? How does it feel? How do you feel?

The only way you will experience the delight, beauty and fulfillment that will come from achieving this goal is if you use your personal initiative. It won't happen without it.

Initiative is a personal power force that rises from the deepest and flows into a positive, goal-oriented activity.

Take action

Your personal initiative is your inner energy that begins to act. It is the enemy of delay. It is the spark that initiates your productive actions. Without personal initiative, one cannot succeed.

Success is something you have to achieve without someone telling you what to do or why you should do it.

Success comes to those who are proactive. Instead of wandering through life doing only

what is needed, successful individuals do the additional things that give life more meaning.

Whatever your goal - to become a remarkable mother, an honor student, a great athlete, a high-production salesman, or the owner of your own business - if you are going to succeed, you must use your personal initiative to do the little things that are required of you in order to succeed.

Personal initiative is more than a rudimentary requirement to achieve your goals, it is also about doing the little things that make your life and other people's lives, both at work and at home, more enjoyable.

It's doing simple things like cleaning your

dirty clothes, cleaning house 12. Or emptying the spill onto the trash can. It takes 3 minutes to clean the coffee cups in the office sink. It is taking time to convey your genuine gratitude to someone who did something for you. It is offered to help a friend in need and is essential for a positive mentality.

In a way, your personal initiative is to observe and be aware of the tasks that need to be done without being asked.

Among my fundamental beliefs is that the only way to have personal initiative to do huge things is to use it first to do small things. Each great success is made up of a large number of small successes, each of which requires personal initiative and many of which are so small and insignificant that you simply notice it, but they all add up.

Using one's own personal initiative has more advantages than can be seen by the naked eye.

Individuals who use their personal initiative are more respected and have greater influence.

No other technique for building self-esteem is more effective than using your personal initiative to do the small tasks that make you a better individual.

The people who constantly use their personal initiative to promote their vocations are those at the top of their profession's pay scale.

You will have the advantage in everything you do, as you will stand out as an individual worthy of being noticed who has a positive mentality.

I am not sure of the cause, but I see fewer people using their personal initiative to advance their lives than at any other time in my life. It's like everyone is sitting in a waiting pattern waiting for something to change.

This is your chance to accelerate your game and distinguish yourself from the growing number of apathetic individuals. This is your opportunity to use your unique talent, ability and power to accomplish the things that are meaningful to you.

Don't let the lethargic environment around you keep you from stretching out to become your best person.

I want to challenge them to start doing the little things that require personal initiative. As you establish your confidence in the execution of the little things, then begin to stretch to do the bigger things. Go ahead with this procedure and let each success build on the previous one.

Self-control

Self-control is the power to make you take action yourself regardless of your emotional state or a way to maintain a positive mental attitude.

Putting it in order

Imagine what you could accomplish if you could only make your best intentions come true no matter what. The pinnacle of self-control is when you get to the point where you come to a conscious decision; it's almost guaranteed that you'll stick with it.

Self-control is one of the many personal development tools available to you.

Naturally it's not a cure. Still, the problems that self-control can solve are crucial, and although there are other ways to solve these problems, self-control destroys them completely.

Self-control can give you the power to erase postponement, maintain a positive mental attitude and be a success. In addition, it becomes a powerful teammate when combined with other tools.

Self-control is like muscle. The more you discipline it, the stronger it becomes. The less discipline, the weaker it becomes.

Just as each person has different muscle strength, we all have different levels of self-control. Everyone has something - if you can hold your breath for a couple of seconds, you have a little self-control. But not everyone has formulated their discipline at the same level.

The way to establish self-control is how to use weight training to establish muscle. This involves lifting weights that are close to your limitations. You force your muscles until they fail, and then you rest.

In the same way, the basic technique for building self-control is to address the challenges that you are able to achieve successfully, but that are close to your limitations. It involves trying something and

failing at it on a daily basis, nor does it involve staying within your comfort zone.

You won't gain strength by trying to lift a weight you can't move, nor will you acquire weightlifting weights that are too weak for you. You have to start with weights/jackets that are within your current ability to lift but that are close to your limitations.

When you succeed, you rise to the challenge. Although most individuals have very weak muscles compared to the strength they can get with training, most individuals are really weak at their level of self-control.

If you are really undisciplined right now, you are able to use the little discipline you have to form more. The more disciplined you get, the easier life becomes. Things that used to be inconceivable to you will now feel like child's play. As you become stronger, the same weights will feel lighter and lighter.

Don't equate yourself with others. It won't do any good. You will only discover what you hope to discover. If you think you are weak, everyone else will feel stronger.

If you think you are strong, everyone else will look weaker. It doesn't make sense to do this. Just consider where you are today and try to improve as you go.

Original vision

The original thought is the creation of something that did not exist before, either as a product, as a procedure or as a thought.

You would be demonstrating an original thought if you:

- Cook something that has never existed before.

- Ideate something that exists elsewhere but you don't know.

- Prepare a new procedure to do something.

- Reapply an existing procedure or product in a new or modified market.

- Formulate a new way of seeing something (bringing a new idea into existence).

- Altering the way someone else sees something.

In fact, we are all original days because we are constantly altering the ideas we have about the world around us. The original thought doesn't have to be about developing something new for the world, but rather about formulating something new for ourselves. Once we alter ourselves, the world alters with us, both in the way the world is impacted by our different actions and in the way we pass through the world.

Be creative

Original thinking can be used to make better products, procedures and services and can be used to produce them in the first place. It is hoped that increasing your original thinking will help you, your organization and your customers to be happier through improvements in your quality and quantity of production.

Original thinking is the procedure we use when we are presented with a new notion. They are the mixture of ideas that have not been mixed before.

Brainstorming is an original way of thinking: it works by mixing the ideas of others with your own to produce a new one. You are

39

using other people's ideas as a stimulus for your own.

This original thought process may be accidental or deliberate.

Without using special strategies, the original thought still happens, but commonly in the accidental form; like a fortuitous event that makes you consider something in a different way and then discover an advantageous change.

Additional changes occur slowly through pure utilization of intelligence and logical advancement. Using this process of accidental or logical advancement, it often takes a long time for products to be formulated and improved. In an increasingly

fast and competitive world, this is clearly detrimental.

Using special strategies, original deliberate thinking can be used to develop new ideas. These strategies force you to combine a wide range of thoughts to trigger new thoughts and procedures. Brainstorming is one of these special strategies, but it traditionally starts with non-original ideas.

Product developments happen much faster using these deliberate strategies than by accident. Many individuals known to be original use these strategies, but are not aware that they are doing so because they have not been officially trained in them. If you use these deliberate strategies during the advanced brainstorming sessions, then you will also be more original, which in turn will add to your positive mental attitude.

With practice, ongoing original thinking (continuous research, questioning and analysis that is developed through education, conditioning and self-awareness) occurs at all times. The original thought in progress maximizes both accidental and deliberate original thinking. Continuing creativity takes time and deliberate practice to achieve full dexterity, but it is amazing how quickly it becomes a mental attitude, not a strategy.

The first step is to learn creative thinking strategies so that you can deliberately use them and have new ideas. Then you will have an immediate advantage over those who don't understand how to use them.

You should then practice strategies to increase your skills in the original ongoing thinking as well as boost your positive mental attitude.

Organized thinking and concentration

Concentration and organized thinking work together, but one does not lead to the other.

To concentrate is to direct your mental forces or your efforts toward a certain action, theme, or matter.

Memory is the power to remember information, experiences and individuals. There are some particular skills that can be learned to increase both concentration and organized thinking.

Practicing these skills is likely to improve one's positive mental attitude.

Put Your Brain in Order

When something is stored in our brain, we don't forget it. However, we may have difficulty re-entering the data. It is also possible that the data we are trying to re-calibrate has never been stored.

Good concentration will increase organized thinking. If we only practice skills that improve our organized thinking but never look at divisors that improve concentration, our efforts will only be marginal and successful.

Make your mind a deal that I cannot refuse. Yes, the mind accepts bribes. Instead of telling it NOT to worry about a different, lower priority (which will cause its brain to consider the same thing it is not supposed to consider), assign it a task with start and stop time parameters.

For example, "I will consider how to pay off that credit card debt when I get home this afternoon and have the opportunity to add up my debts. From 1-1:30 pm, I will provide my total focus to the practice of this presentation, so I am eloquent and articulate when I launch this proposal.

Still can't get other concerns out of your brain? Write them on your to-do list so you can block them. Registering distressing obligations means you don't have to use your brain as a "reminder" message board, which means you are able to give your full attention to your main priority task.

Don't you feel like concentrating? Are you dodging a task or project you're supposed to be working on? That's kind of procrastination. It's amazing how long it takes to finish something we're not working on.

Next time you're about to postpone an obligation, ask yourself, "Do I have to do this? Do I want it to be fulfilled so it's not in my mind? Will it be simpler later?"

Those 3 questions can provide the incentive for you to apply yourself mentally as you face the reality that this task is not disappearing, and the delay will simply add to your feelings of guilt and make this heavy task take up more of your brain and time.

Imagine your brain as a camera and your eyes as your opening. Most of the time, our eyes are "assimilating" and our mind is in "wide-angle focus". We can consider a lot of things at once and maneuver realistically and efficiently in this way.

What if you want to switch to the telephoto focus? What if you have to prepare for a test and need 100% concentration? Put your hands over your eyes so there's

"Tunnel vision" and they're just looking at your text. Place your hands on the sides of the face screens so that they are literally "hidden, out of the mind. Consider the importance of those words.

If you put your hands over your eyes every time you want to switch from a wide-angle to a telephoto approach, that physical ritual becomes a Pavlovian trigger.

Using your hands as intermittent each time you want to narrow your focus teaches your mind to switch to "one track" of the mind and focus on your command.

Do you want to know how to be "present" and full here and now instead of running aimlessly here, there and everywhere? The next time your brain is a million miles away, just look around and truly see your surroundings. Study that delicate flower in the vase. Approach the image of the wall and marvel at the artist's craftsmanship.

Support yourself and truly see a loved one you tend to take for granted. Your world will come alive in the eye of your mind.

Budgeting time and being enthusiastic

If time is a non-renewable resource, it is added together to make the most of the time presented to you. Learn how to set a budget and maximize the time you have.

Let life vanish without a clear, defined and determined purpose. Now you have the pure formula for boredom!

If you let the day go by without enthusiasm and vigour, you're opening holes for dull moments and negative mentality to take over.

Time

When it comes to devising purchases, many individuals have an idea in their brains of what they are willing to spend. I probably wouldn't walk into a shoe store and say, 'I'll buy that pair of shoes no matter how much they cost.

If the seller states that the shoes cost $300, most individuals would not buy them.

That's because when it comes to shopping, people budget in their brains how much those shoes are really worth to them.

But what happens when it comes to how you

spend your time?

Do you spend more time on particular tasks than they are really worth?

For example, when it comes to house cleaning, do you spend 60 minutes a day doing it?

2 hours? 3 hours? More than 3 hours? Is it worth dusting for so long?

What about their projects and additional assignments? How much is that time worth to you?

We all have the same sum of time every day,

24 hours. At least eight of those hours go to sleep. So, we have about sixteen hours when we're awake.

By arranging a time budget for particular activities, you will always ensure that your time is spent on what is most crucial to you, your loved ones and your future.

How much time do you want to invest with your spouse or love? How many hours will you spend working, cleaning, exercising, eating, or watching TV?

Before you organize something, ask yourself how much time you are willing to spend. Put in those time investments so you can refer to them regularly. Then stick to your time budget.

Time is not an inexhaustible currency, so be sure to spend it wisely.

Emotion

Go somewhere you've never been. Anything fresh will make your brain feel curious and invigorated. This raises the clumsiness of your current way of life. Fresh places give you back the childlike curiosity in you. Curiosity keeps you alive; and traveling is, from afar and afar, the best antidote to boredom.

It is often said that: "All work and no play is a boring day. You have to work to be able to pay the bills. Similarly, working without fun from time to time can result in apathy.

Once a year, take time to go to a cool place or alien land (if your budget allows) and add fresh information to your electronic intelligence vault.

If you're a pet lover, drive to a pet store of your choice and choose a pet. Individuals claim that dogs are the most sincere companions. You've heard that dogs risk their lives for their owners.

If you can't keep pets at home, an alternative is to have plants. Others find it healing by talking with orchids, roses and every imaginable flower in the plant kingdom. The flowers in various tones, and the color green, can be relaxing to the eye.

If you have a green thumb, why not try this hobby? If you're excited when you're surrounded by plants, go ahead and grab your horticultural tools!

Boring life can be made exciting through food! Aside from being the source of power (and extra pounds!), use food to make life stimulating. Be on the lookout for fresh food ideas through food and the distinction of unique restaurants.

Think of cooking as a different activity that can stimulate mood. Cooking exposes you to a variety of flavors and textures of ingredients. Who knows? You may be looking for a business adventure in the future if you indulge your passion for cooking.

Distinguish what you want and love to accomplish. If you're not at it by now, this is the ideal time to begin the discovery process. Perhaps now is the right time to learn a new skill like playing an instrument, joining a gym and acquiring new habits.

This will do wonders for your life in terms of physical well-being and elimination of boredom.

Other people do volunteer work. This is a different alternative that certainly satisfies and uplifts the spirit.

In all of these actions, you can invite like-minded acquaintances to join you on your journey. The moment you decide to pursue a clear and definite purpose and do something that gives meaning to your life, you have taken the initial step toward a life of relentless fulfillment and a positive mental attitude.

Final thoughts

This is the initial step.... reading. It should be a quick read, to capture the broad flow of thought that the book carries.

Read for some emphasis. A second reading is intended to absorb particular details. You must pay some attention to make sure that you really understand and grasp any new ideas that the book presents.

Read for the future. This third reading is more of an organized thought feat than a reading job. You will literally learn passages that have some meaning to you.

Discover ways they can relate to the problems you are currently facing. Try fresh ideas; try them; discard what is not worthwhile; and imprint what is valuable indelibly on your habit patterns.

Read - later - to review your memory, and to rekindle your inspiration. There's a famous story about the salesman standing in front of a sales manager who says: "Give me that old sales talk again, I'm getting discouraged. All of us could be discouraged. We should reread the best of our books at that time to rekindle the fires that set us in motion at the initial place.

Visit our author page on Amazon and get more MENTES LIBRES!

http://amazon.com/author/menteslibres

If you wish, you can leave a comment on this book by clicking on the following link so that we can continue to grow! Thank you very much for your purchase!

https://www.amazon.com/dp/B082LT9RQ7

Made in the USA
Middletown, DE
12 January 2023

21974673R00035